Cameron Mackintosh presents
The Theatre Royal Stratford East Production of

FIVE GUYS
NAMED MOE

STOW·COLLEGE
43 SHAMROCK STREET
GLASGOW   G4 9LD
TELEPHONE: 0141·332·1786
FACSIMILE: 0141·332·5207

Music
Theatre

Vocal selections from the musical by Clarke Peters.

Wise Publications
London/New York/Sydney

3230019466

Five Guys Named Moe

Words & Music by Larry Wynn & Jerry Bresler

four eyed___ Moe,_____

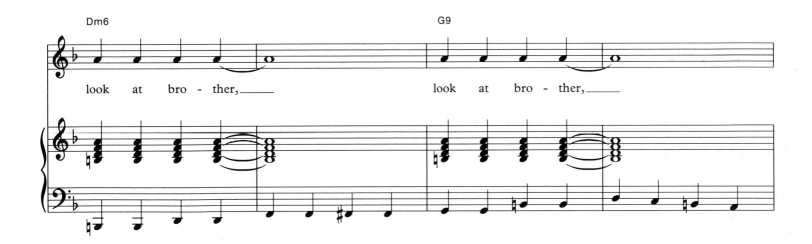

no Moe,___

look at bro - ther,_____ look at bro - ther,_____

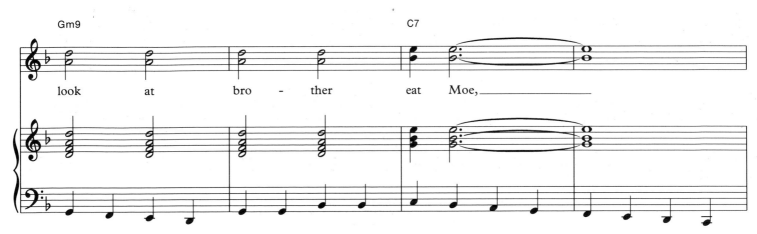

look at bro - ther eat Moe,_____

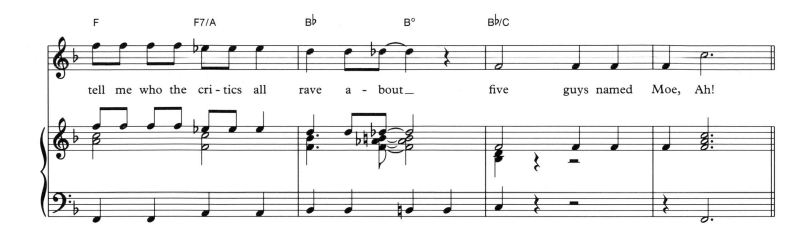

tell me who the cri - tics all rave a - bout_ five guys named Moe, Ah!

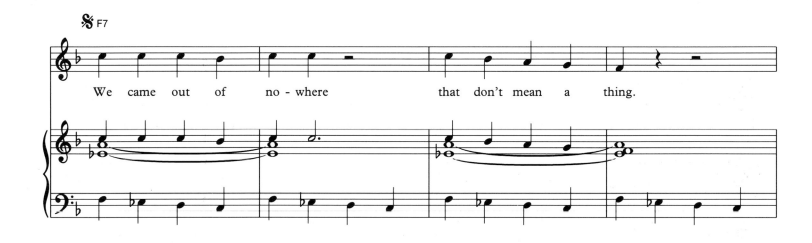

We came out of no - where that don't mean a thing.

We rate high_ and you'll know why_ when you hear us sing,_____

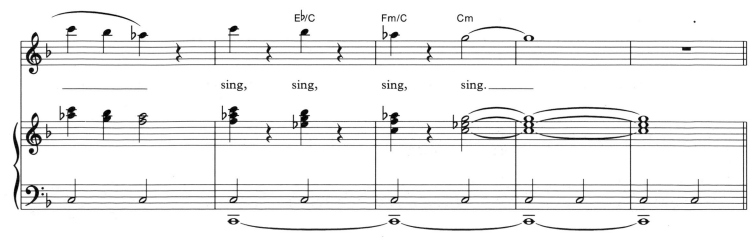

_____ sing, sing, sing, sing._____

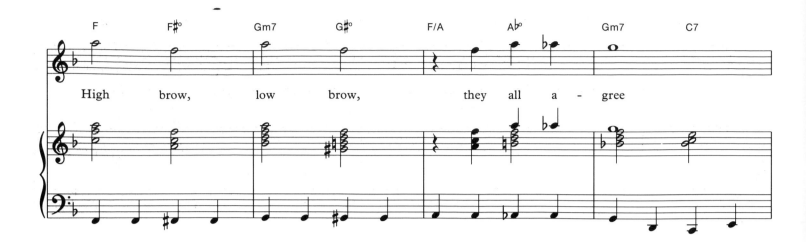

High brow, low brow, they all a-gree

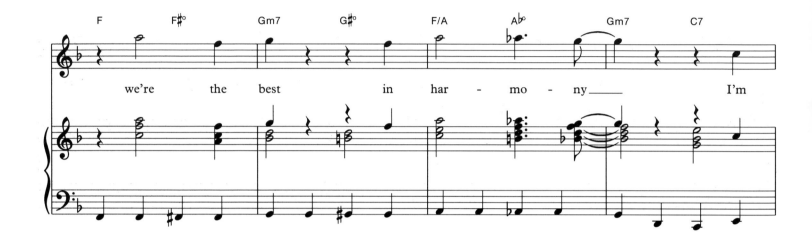

we're the best in har-mo-ny_____ I'm

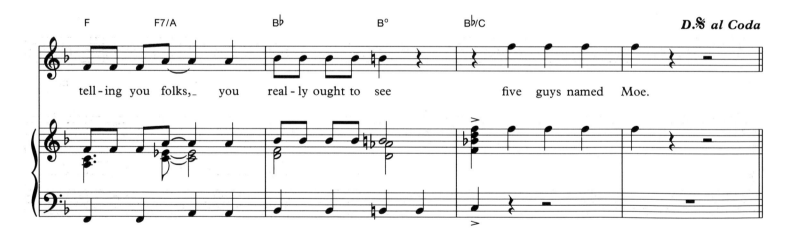

D.$.al Coda

tell-ing you folks,_ you real-ly ought to see five guys named Moe.

CODA

sing._____

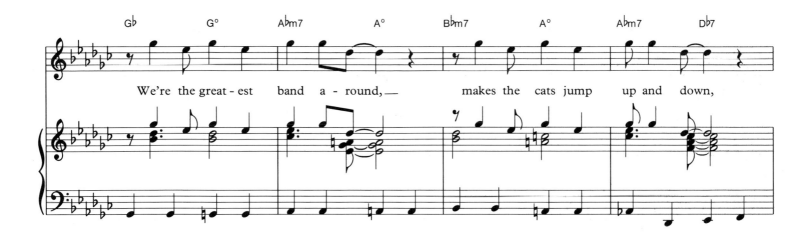

We're the great-est band a-round,__ makes the cats jump up and down,

we're the talk of rhy-thm town,__ five guys named Moe. Not

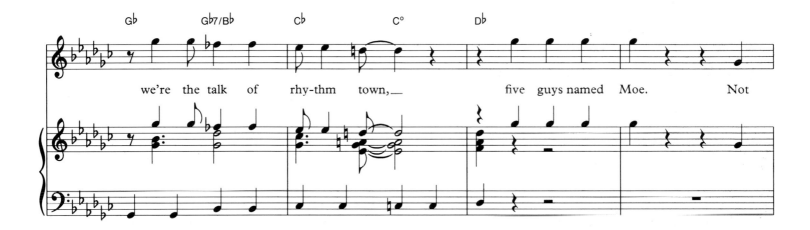

one guy,__ (No Moe) not

two guys,__ (Little Biddy Moe) not

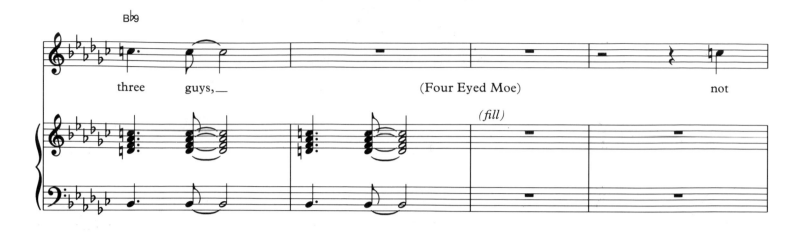

three guys,___ (Four Eyed Moe) not

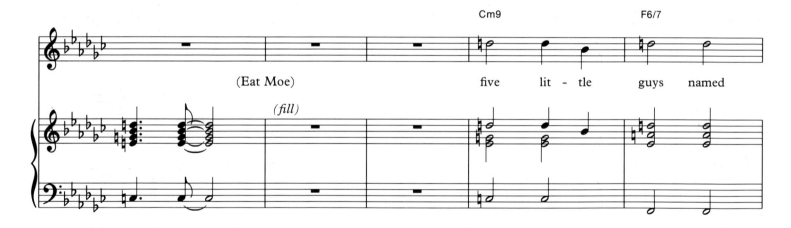

four guys,___ (Big Moe) but five guys,___

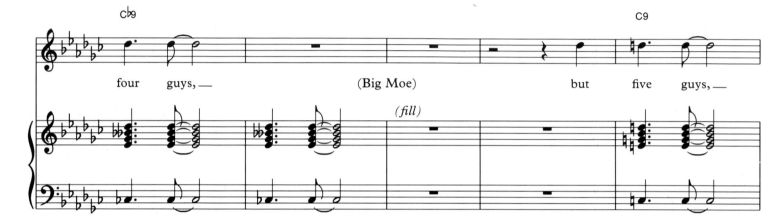

(Eat Moe) five lit - tle guys named

Moe,_____ that's us.
Moe,_____
Moe,_____
Moe,_____
Moe,

Messy Bessy

Words & Music by Jimmy Smith

and this is what you'll hear me say.

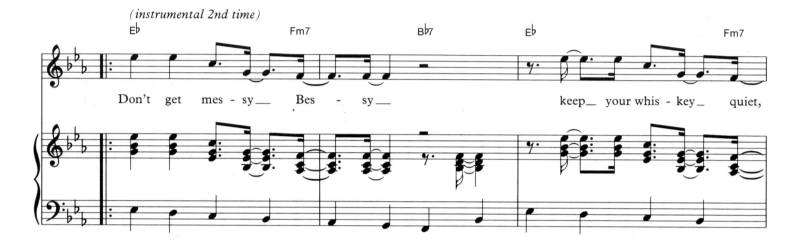

(instrumental 2nd time)

Don't get mes - sy__ Bes - sy__ keep__ your whis - key__ quiet,

when you had__ a cou-ple of drinks_____ wo - man,

you just might__ start a riot.__ Don't get mes - sy__ Bes -

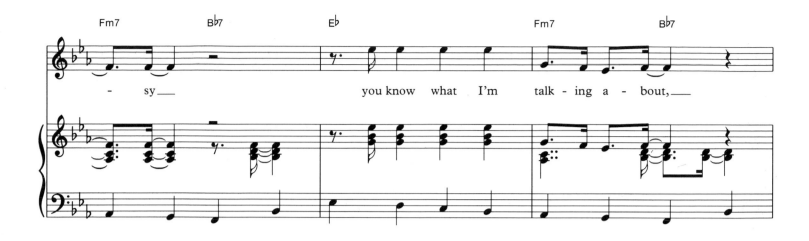

-sy___ you know what I'm talk-ing a-bout,___

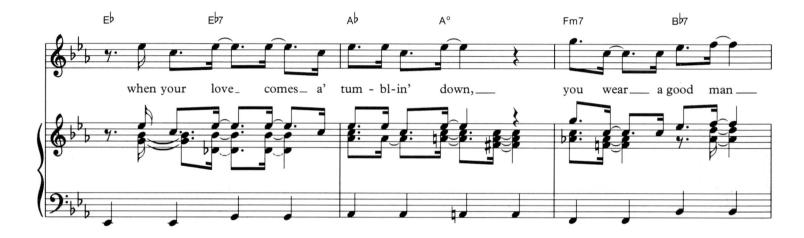

when your love_ comes_ a' tum-bl-in' down,___ you wear_ a good man___

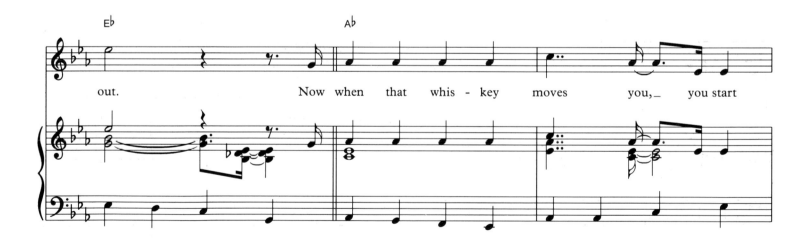

out. Now when that whis-key moves you,_ you start

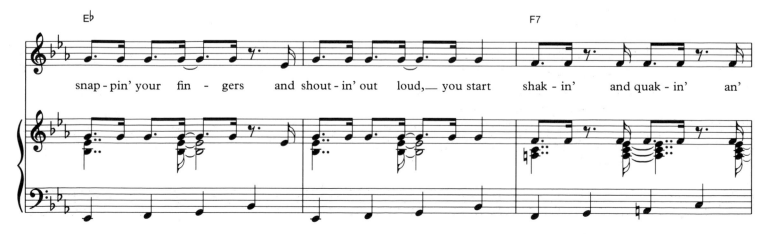

snap-pin' your fin - gers and shout-in' out loud,_ you start shak-in' and quak-in' an'

whoop-in' and hol-ler-in', you talk so loud you draw a crowd, { So / now }

don't get mes-sy Bes-sy, try to play it cool,

'cause you just wait till I get you home ma-ma, and

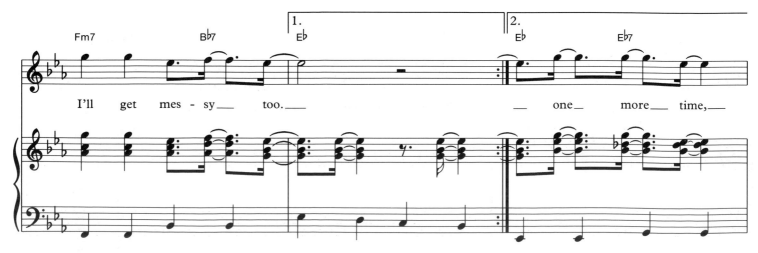

I'll get mes-sy too. one more time,

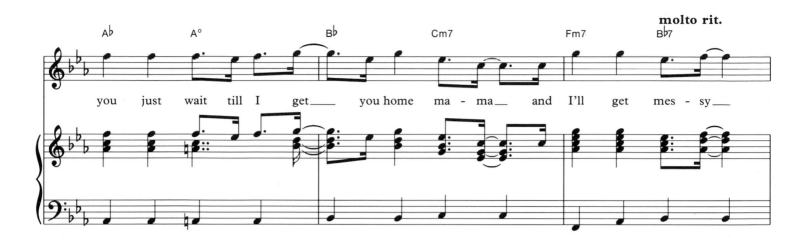

you just wait till I get___ you home ma - ma___ and I'll get mes - sy___

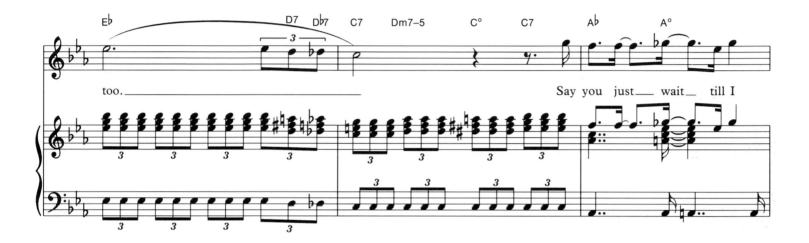

too._____ Say you just___ wait___ till I

get you home ma - ma,___ and I'll get___ mes - sy___ too._____

_____ You bet-ter straigh-ten up and fly right wo-man.

I Like 'Em Fat Like That

Words & Music by Claude Demetrius, Louis Jordan & J. Mayo Williams

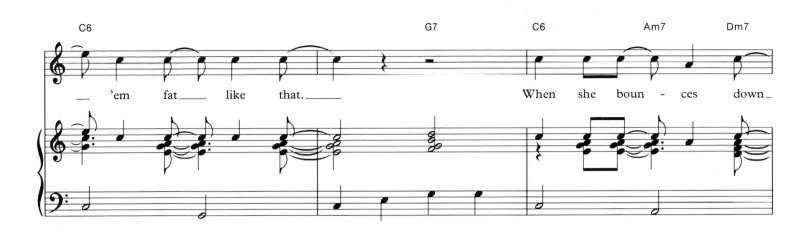

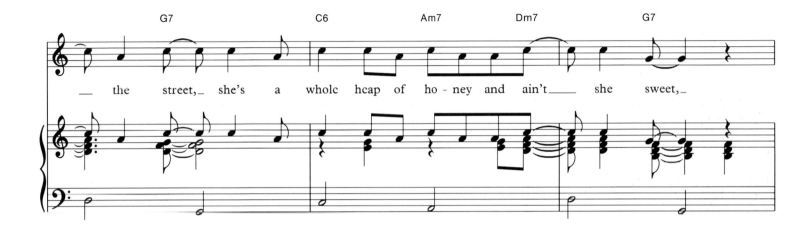

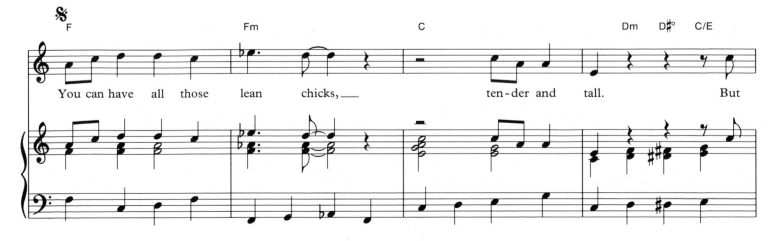

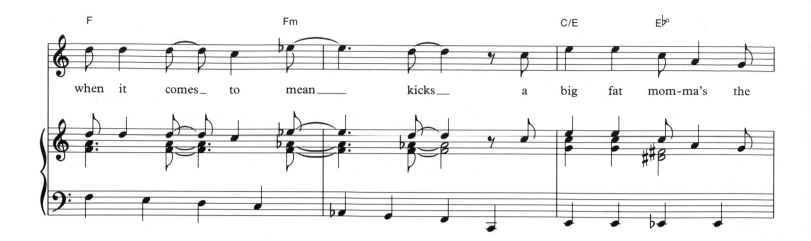

when it comes_ to mean___ kicks__ a big fat mom-ma's the

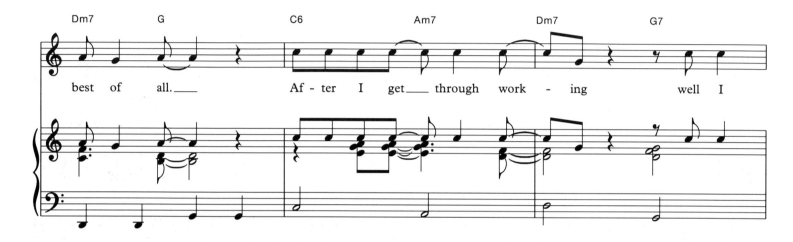

best of all.___ Af - ter I get__ through work - ing well I

reach and I grab__ my hat,___ and I hur - ry home,_ don't want her__

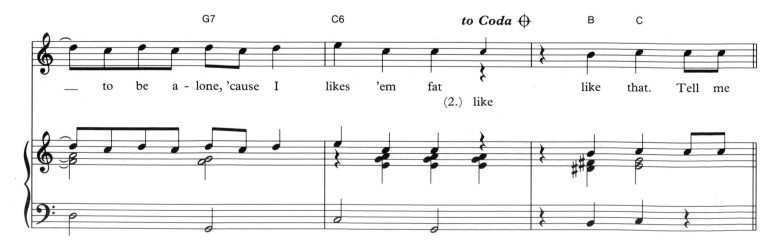

__ to be a - lone, 'cause I likes 'em fat like that. Tell me

(2.) like

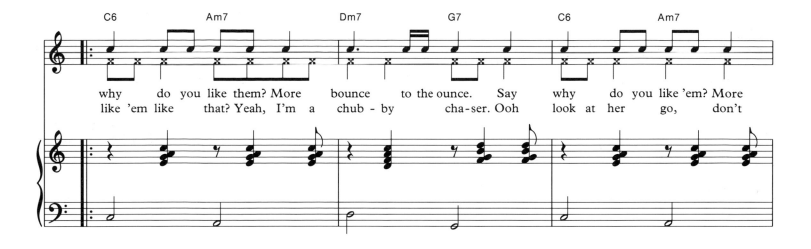

why   do you like them? More   bounce   to the ounce. Say   why   do you like 'em? More
like 'em like   that? Yeah, I'm a   chub - by   cha - ser. Ooh   look at her   go,   don't

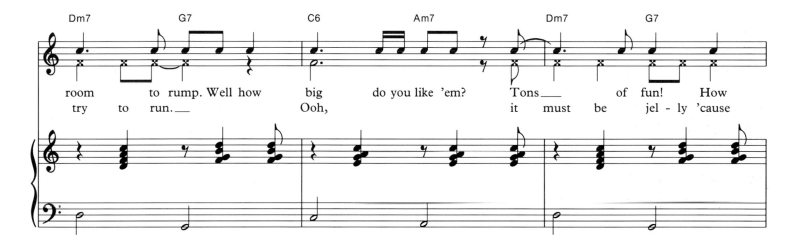

room   to rump. Well how   big   do you like 'em?   Tons___   of fun!   How
try   to run. ___   Ooh,   it must be   jel - ly 'cause

1.
C6   G7   2.
C6   D.%

wide   do you like 'em?   Well like   that. So you   jam don't shake   like   that.

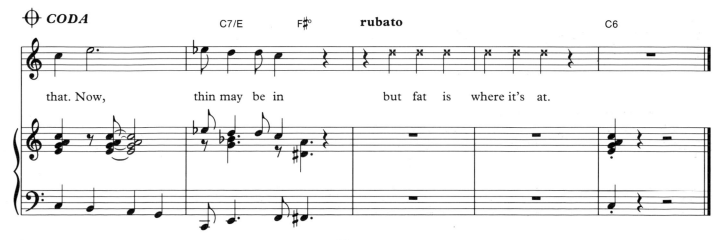

⊕ CODA   C7/E   F#°   **rubato**   C6

that. Now,   thin may be in   but fat is   where it's at.

Safe, Sane And Single

Words & Music by Johnny Lange, Hy Heath & Louis Jordan

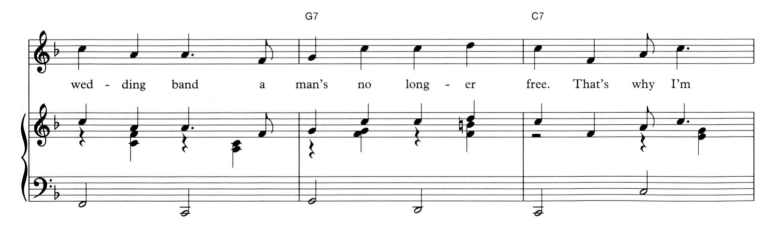

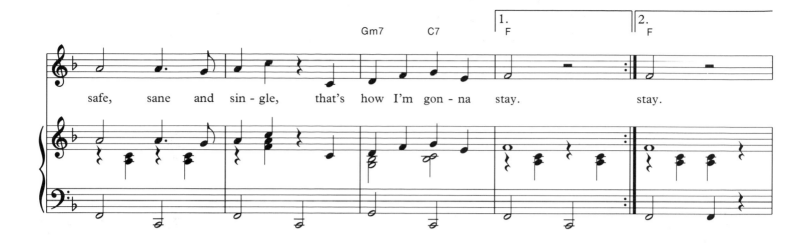

safe, sane and sin - gle, that's how I'm gon - na stay. stay.

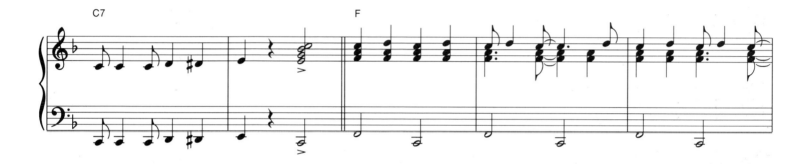

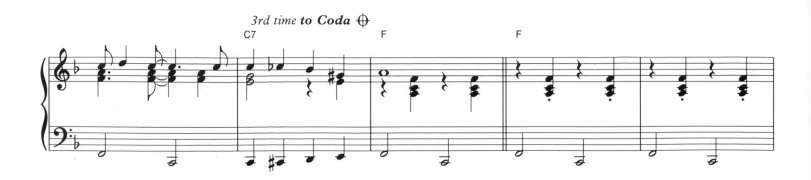

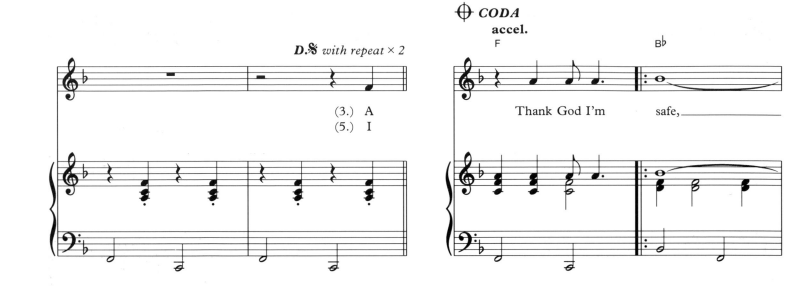

gon - na stay.＿＿＿＿＿＿＿＿＿ Hey!

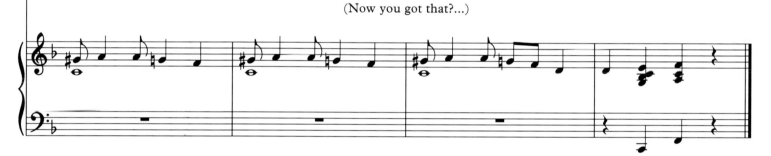

(Now you got that?...)

Verse 2
A wife and husband came upon
The parting of their ways;
The judge gave her the bank account
and gave him 90 days.

That's why I'm safe,... *etc.*

Verse 3
A friend of mine got married
To a gal named Nellie Grey;
She pawned his watch, then sold his car
and gave his clothes away.

That's why I'm safe,... *etc.*

Verse 4
I met a gal in Birmingham
and thereby hangs a tale;
She had a husband doing time,
Another out on bail.

That's why I'm safe,... *etc.*

Verse 5
I courted a gal for 15 years,
Her pa said we should wed;
If my horse could only cook
I'd marry him instead.

That's why I'm safe,... *etc.*

PUSH KA PI SHEE PIE

Words & Music by J. Willoughby, L. Jordan & W. Merrick

Push ka pi shee pie eh___ eh,

push ka pi shee pie eh___ eh,   oob li aay ee eye yay ab - la,

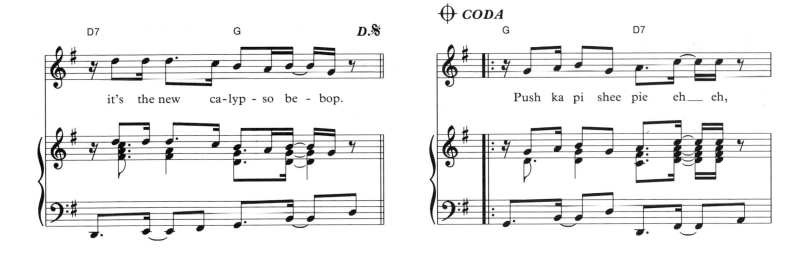

Verse 2
Saigo met a girl in town,
She said she would show him round.
He said 'It's a privilege',
So she sold him the Brooklyn Bridge.
Then she took him to a show,
They land up in the last row.
Saigo ask her for a kiss,
But all she said to him was this:

Push ka pi shi... *etc.*

Verse 3
Saigo asked to take her home,
Thinking that she live alone.
But when Saigo reach the door,
This is what poor Saigo saw.
A shadow of a great big man,
Something shining in his hand.
He no wait to say goodbye,
And as he ran I heard him cry:

Push ka pi shi... *etc.*

Verse 4 (D.S.)
This here push ka pi shi pie,
Makes me laugh until I cry,
Funny thing is that it seems,
No one knows just what it means.

What's The Use Of Gettin' Sober

Words & Music by Busbey Meyers

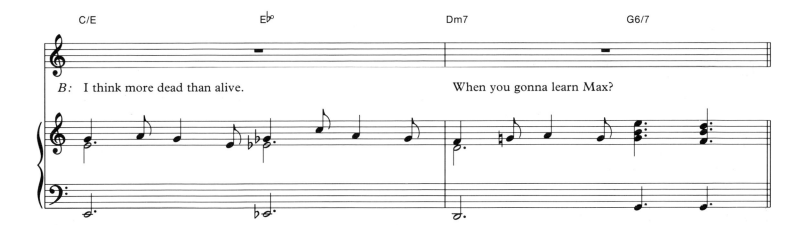

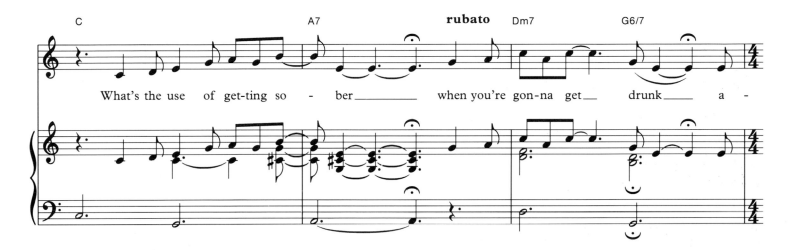

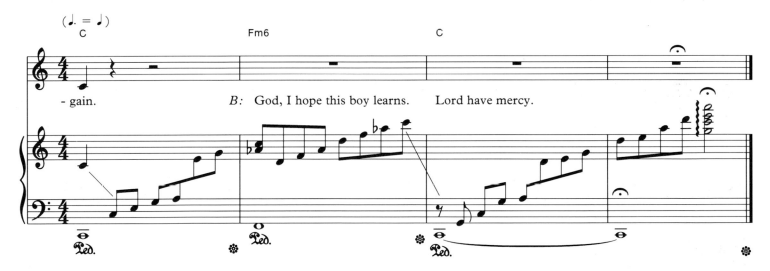

2nd time

Nomax:
Exactly.
You know, Old Sam did something mighty fine
When he brought back good whiskey, beer and wine;
Because I love my whiskey and I love my gin
Every time you see me I'll be in the sin.

Big Moe:
Don't you think you already deep enough in sin?
When you gonna learn Max?

LIFE IS SO PECULIAR

Words by Johnny Burke. Music by Jimmy Van Heusen

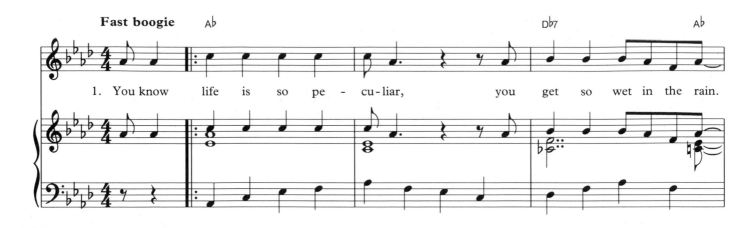

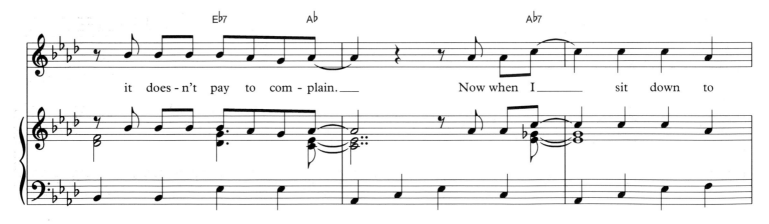

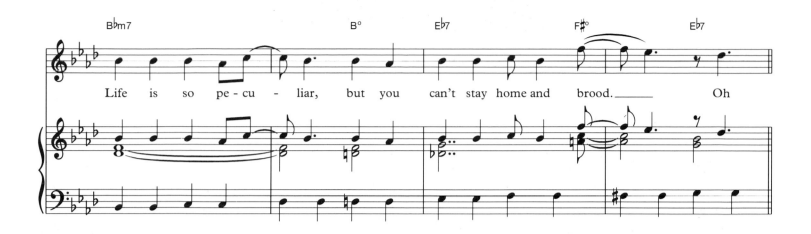

Life is so pe - cu - liar, but you can't stay home and brood._____ Oh

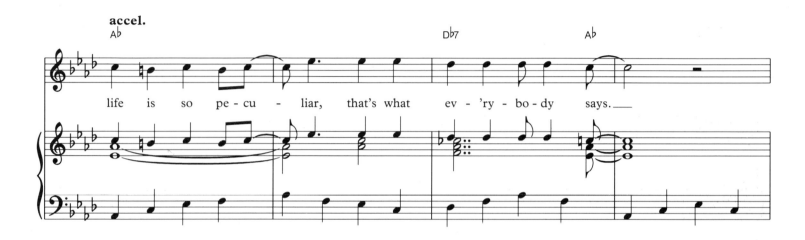

accel.

life is so pe - cu - liar, that's what ev - 'ry - bo - dy says._____

Life is so pe - cu - liar, so don't let a - ny - bo - dy fool____ ya. (2.) Yeah

(3.) Well when

- liar _____ Life is so pe - cu - liar, that's what ev - 'ry - bo - dy says.

Verse 2
Yeah life is so peculiar,
A fork belongs with a knife.
Corn beef is lost without cabbage,
Every husband should have a wife.

Now when I go out to dinner,
There is nothing to wear but clothes.
Whenever I feel sleepy,
There is nothing to do but doze.

Verse 3
Well when I get tired of sitting,
There's nothing to do but walk.
    (Walk on)
When I don't wanna listen,
There's nothing to do but talk.
    (Talk too much)

Whenever I feel thirsty,
There's nothing to do but drink.
    (Oh oh)
Life is so peculiar,
That it makes you stop and think.

CAL'DONIA

Words & Music by Claude Moine & Fleecy Moore

and I love — her just the same.   I'm cra - zy 'bout that wo-man, Cal -

- 'don - ia is her name.   (Here we go!)   Cal - 'don-ia!   What?   Cal - 'don-ia?   What?

Chorus

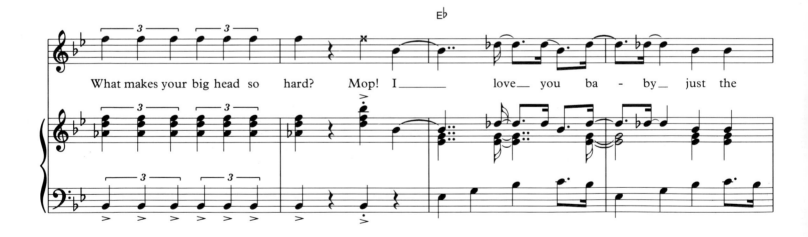

What makes your big head so   hard?   Mop!   I _____ love _ you ba - by _ just the

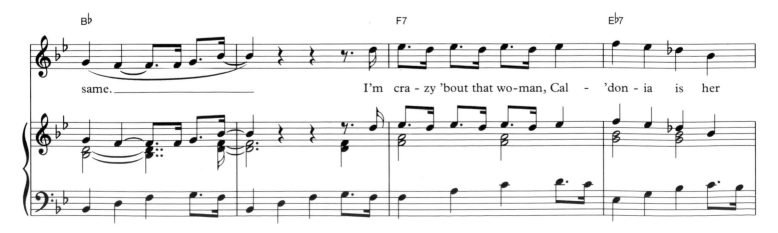

same. _____   I'm cra - zy 'bout that wo-man, Cal - 'don - ia is her

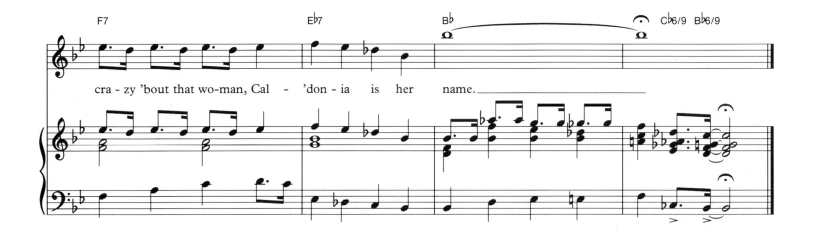

Second time, spoken:
Know what? My momma called me up and she said
'Son, this woman called Cal'donia who you so in love with
All she gonna do is break your heart and take your money',
But you see momma didn't know just what Cal'donia was putting down,
But I tell you what I'm gonna do, I'm gonna go over to her house
And this is what I'm gonna say.

THERE AIN'T NOBODY HERE BUT US CHICKENS

Words & Music by Joan Witney & Alex Kramer

Fast swing

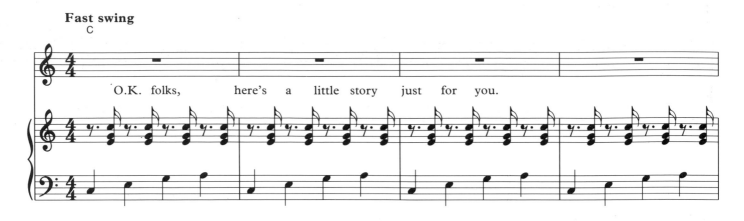

O.K. folks, here's a little story just for you.

Now one night farmer Brown was taking the air; he locked up the farmyard with the greatest of care.

But down in the henhouse, something stirred; and when he shouted 'who's there?' this is what he heard. There

ain't no-bo-dy here but us chick-ens,___ there ain't no-bo-dy here at all.___ So___

quiet your-self_ and stop that fuss,__ there ain't no-bo-dy here but us.__ We chick-ens

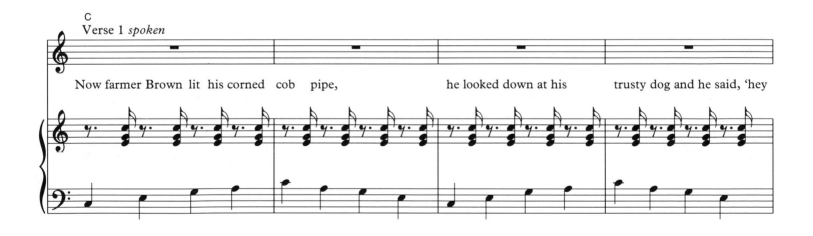

tryin' to sleep__ and you butt in__ and hob-ble hob-ble hob-ble hob-ble it's a sin.

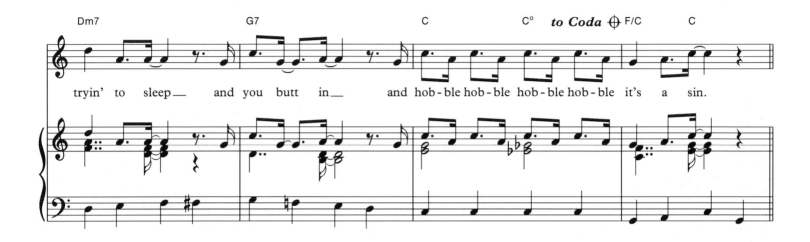

Verse 1 *spoken*

Now farmer Brown lit his corned cob pipe, he looked down at his trusty dog and he said, 'hey

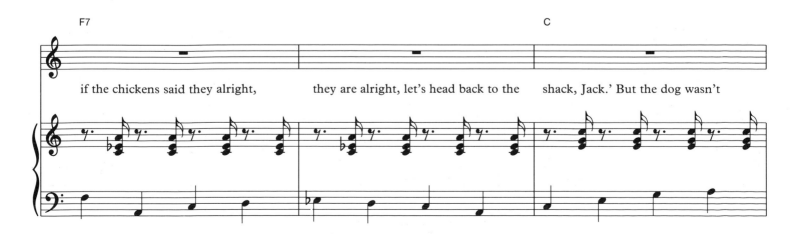

if the chickens said they alright, they are alright, let's head back to the shack, Jack.' But the dog wasn't

convinced, he said 'go back to the henhouse', gave a little doggy knock, and in his

best chickenese said 'is everything alright?' I said there no! To-

-mor-row___ is a bu-sy___ day___ we got things___ to do, we got eggs to lay,___

D.%. al Coda

ground to dig, we got worms to scratch, you know it takes a lot of sit-tin' get-tin' chicks to hatch, be-sides there

Chorus 2
I said there ain't nobody here but us chickens,
There ain't nobody here at all.
You're stompin' around and checkin' around
And kickin' up an awful fuss.
We chickens tryin' to sleep, and you butt in
And hobble hobble hobble hobble it's a sin.

Verse 2
'Okay okay okay' said the dog and he turned to leave,
Just then a very unchickenlike sneeze came
from the henhouse, atchoo
Farmer Brown cocked his gun, he says 'I'm a comin' in,
You better open that door just a little teeny weeny
Bit, so I can take a peek'.

Chorus 3
There ain't nobody here but us chickens,
There ain't nobody here at all.
So stop that fuss and raisin' dust
Hey there ain't nobody here but us.
So kindly point that gun the other way
And hobble hobble hobble off and hit the hay.

Don't Let The Sun Catch You Crying

Words & Music by Joe Greene

You can cry, cry, cry, I

know that you know how to wail, and you can beat your head on the pave-

to Coda ⊕
D.S. al Coda

-ment, un-til the man comes and throws you in jail. (3.) But
(⊕) But

⊕ *CODA*

Don't let the sun catch you cry - ing, cry - ing round my front door.

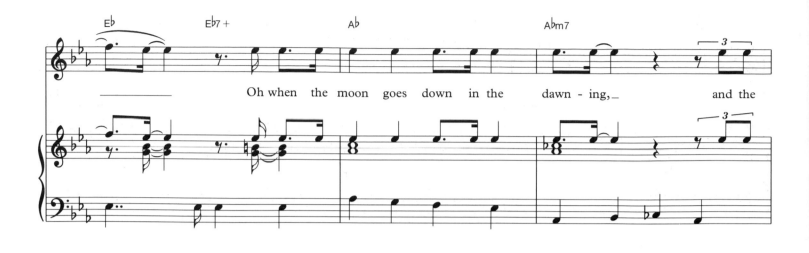

Oh when the moon goes down in the dawn - ing,_ and the

sun comes up in the morn - ing,_ don't let the sun catch you cry - ing._

When the moon goes down in the dawn - ing,_ don't let the

sun catch you cry - ing, 'cause ba - by don't want_ you no_ more,_

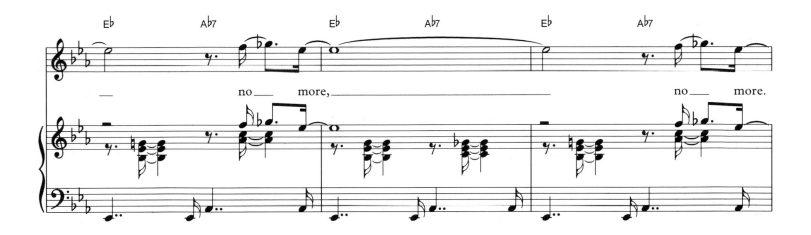

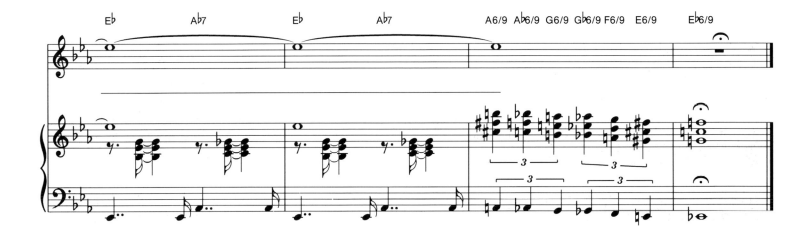

Verse 2
And don't let the sun catch you lyin',
Lyin' round my front door.
Your baby done gone and turned salty,
And you know you made her do so.

Verse 3 (D.S.)
But don't let the sun catch you cryin',
Cryin' round my front door.
You done your baby so dirty,
That's why she don't want you no more.

Middle (D.S.)
Cry and wail,
And you can beat your head on the pavement,
Till the man comes and throws you in jail
– to coda –

Choo Choo Ch' Boogie

Words & Music by Vaughn Horton, Denver Darling & Milt Gabler

Fast boogie

All aboard!

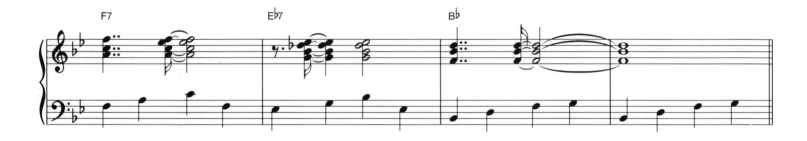

1. Head-in' for the sta-tion with a pack on my back,____ I'm tired of trans-por-ta-tion in the

back of a hack,____ I'd love to hear the rhy-thm of the click-e-ty clack,____ and

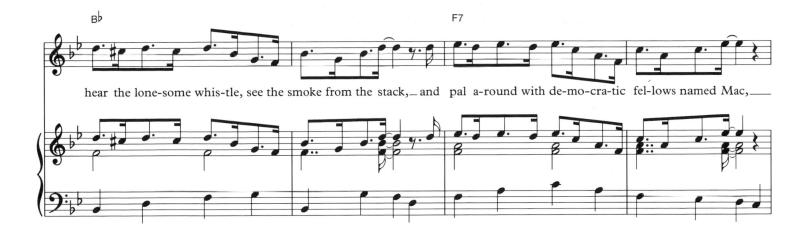

hear the lone-some whis-tle, see the smoke from the stack,__ and pal a-round with de-mo-cra-tic fel-lows named Mac,__

take me right back to the track,__ Jack.__ Choo_ choo_____ choo_ choo ch'boo-gie, Woo

__ woo_____ woo_ woo ch'boo-gie, Choo_ choo_____ choo_ choo ch'boo-gie,

1.2.

take me right back to the track, Jack.__ (2.) You take me right back to the track, Jack.
(3.) I'm

3.

Take__ me,_____ take__ me,_____

I'm__ head - ing for the sta - tion,___ and I need
Yeah, I'll reach__ my des - ti - na - tion,___ and I need

__ some trans - por - ta - tion,___ take__ me,_____ So I reach__ my des - ti - na - tion,___
__ some com - pen - sa - tion,___ So I read__ the si - tu - a - tions,___

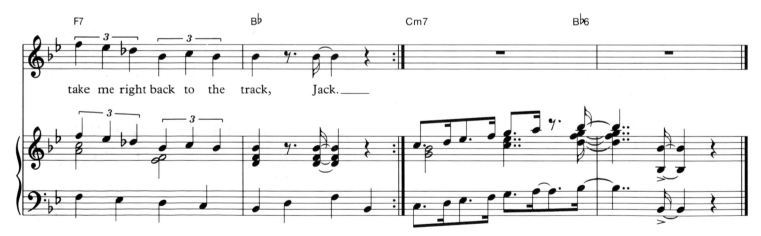

take me right back to the track, Jack.___

Verse 2
You reach your destination but alas and alack,
You need some compensation to get back in the black,
You take a morning paper from the top of the stack,
And read the situations from the front to the back,
The only job that's open needs a man with a knack,
So put it right back in the rack, Jack.

Verse 3
I'm gonna settle down by the railroad track,
Live the life of Reilly in a beaten down shack,
So when I hear the whistle I can peep through the crack,
And watch the train a' rolling when it's balling the jack,
For I just love the rhythm of the clickety clack,
So take me right back to the track... now.

IS YOU IS, OR IS YOU AN'T (MA' BABY)

Words & Music by Billy Austin & Louis Jordan

friends say I could do a lot bet-ter,___ if this keeps up I'll soon need a nurse.___ I

know I can't do a-ny bet-ter,___ but be-lieve me I could do a lot worse.___

Is___ you is or is you ain't my ba-by?___ The

way you're act-ing late-ly makes me doubt.___

Is___ you is or is you ain't my ba - by?___

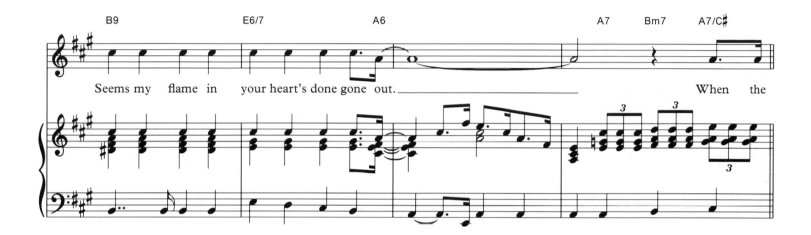

Seems my flame in your heart's done gone out.___ When the

moon goes down in the dawn - ing___ and the sun comes up in the morn -

- ing,___ don't let the sun catch you cry - in'. When the

moon goes down in the dawn - ing,___ don't let the sun catch you cry - in' if your

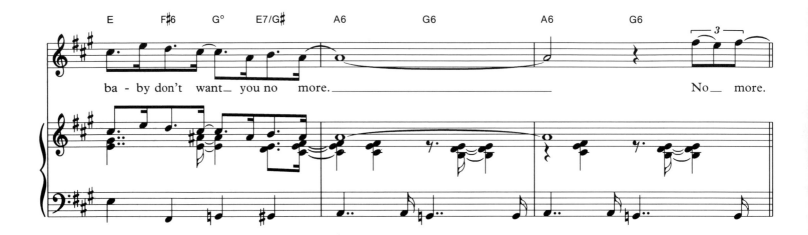

ba - by don't want___ you no more._____ No___ more.

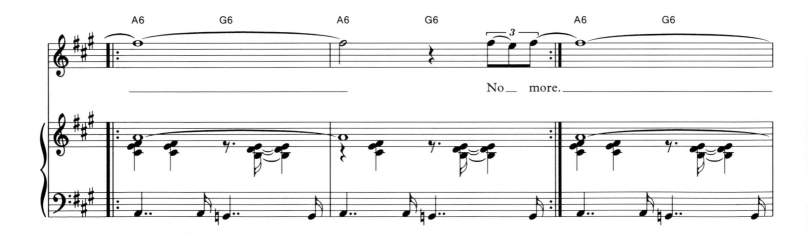

_____ No___ more._____